BOLD KIDS

CHILDREN'S BOOK FILLED WITH FACTS

No part of this book may be reproduced or used in any way or form or by any means whether electronic or mechanical, this means that you cannot record or photocopy any material ideas or tips that are provided in this book.
Copyright 2022

All images in this book have been reproduced with the knowledge and prior consent of the artists concerned, and no responsibility is accepted by producer, publisher, or printer for any infringement of copyright or otherwise, arising from the contents of this publication.

When it comes to learning about the state of Wyoming, there are many different things to learn. This book will cover the history of the state, the famous buffalo, and its role in establishing voting rights for all people.

With pictures and information about the various symbols of Wyoming, it will be easy to discover interesting facts about this western state. This is one of the best ways to teach kids about this unique and beautiful state. There are several fun facts to learn about this state.

The state is aptly nicknamed the Cowboy State because it celebrates the rodeo, the state sport. During Cheyenne Frontier Days, which began in 1897, people can enjoy bull riding, country concerts, and rodeos. Another fun fact about Wyoming is that it can pack in snow.

In the winter of 1979–80, the city of Cheyenne, for example, received 121.5 inches of snow. The state experienced rapid growth between 1870 and 1910. Between those two dates, the population increased by 16 times. Since that time, the population of Wyoming has increased by almost 418,000.

The state's capital city, Cheyenne, is the state's largest city. The state has a small population, but the capital is the largest. It is located in Laramie County and is one of the least centrally located capitals in the U.S.

A number of fun facts about Wyoming can be found in this state. Its famous buffalo, antelope, and elk are just some of the many colorful characters that live here.

The state's state capital is Cheyenne. It is the most populous city in the state, and it's also the least centrally located. The capital is not in the center of the state, so it's a great place for children to learn about the state's rich history.

There are many fun facts about Wyoming that you can share with your child during his or her next geography or U.S. history class.

The state capital is Cheyenne. It is located in Laramie County and is the most populated city in Wyoming. Despite its small size, Wyoming has a rich history that will inspire your children. With this information, they'll be able to learn more about the state's state flag and national parks.

The Wyoming capital has also been known for its pioneering role in women's rights. Its famous parks and natural wonders are not the only things that you can teach about Wyoming.

The state's capital is Cheyenne. It is the most populous city in the state and is the state's most centrally located. However, it is one of the most isolated capitals in the U.S. It is the most western state.

And the only major city in the state is Cheyenne. In contrast, other cities are more populous. Hence, it is best to introduce kids to Wyoming's history and culture by showing them pictures of the capital of the state.

If you are teaching children about the state of Wyoming, you can give them information about the animals. The bison is the official state animal of Wyoming. They are not the only animals that are native to the state, but they are also the most common mammals.

They are the only mammals in the U.S. that are not considered migratory. The population of the bison is approximately six million. The average population of the bison is lower than the population of any other state.

For kids, Wyoming is one of the states with the least population. Nonetheless, it has a rich history. In addition to being the state's least populous, it also boasts some of the most spectacular scenery in the country.

There are many fascinating facts about this state for kids to enjoy. And because it is the least populous state in the United States, it is an ideal location for students. And it is also an important place to learn about the early progressivism of the region.

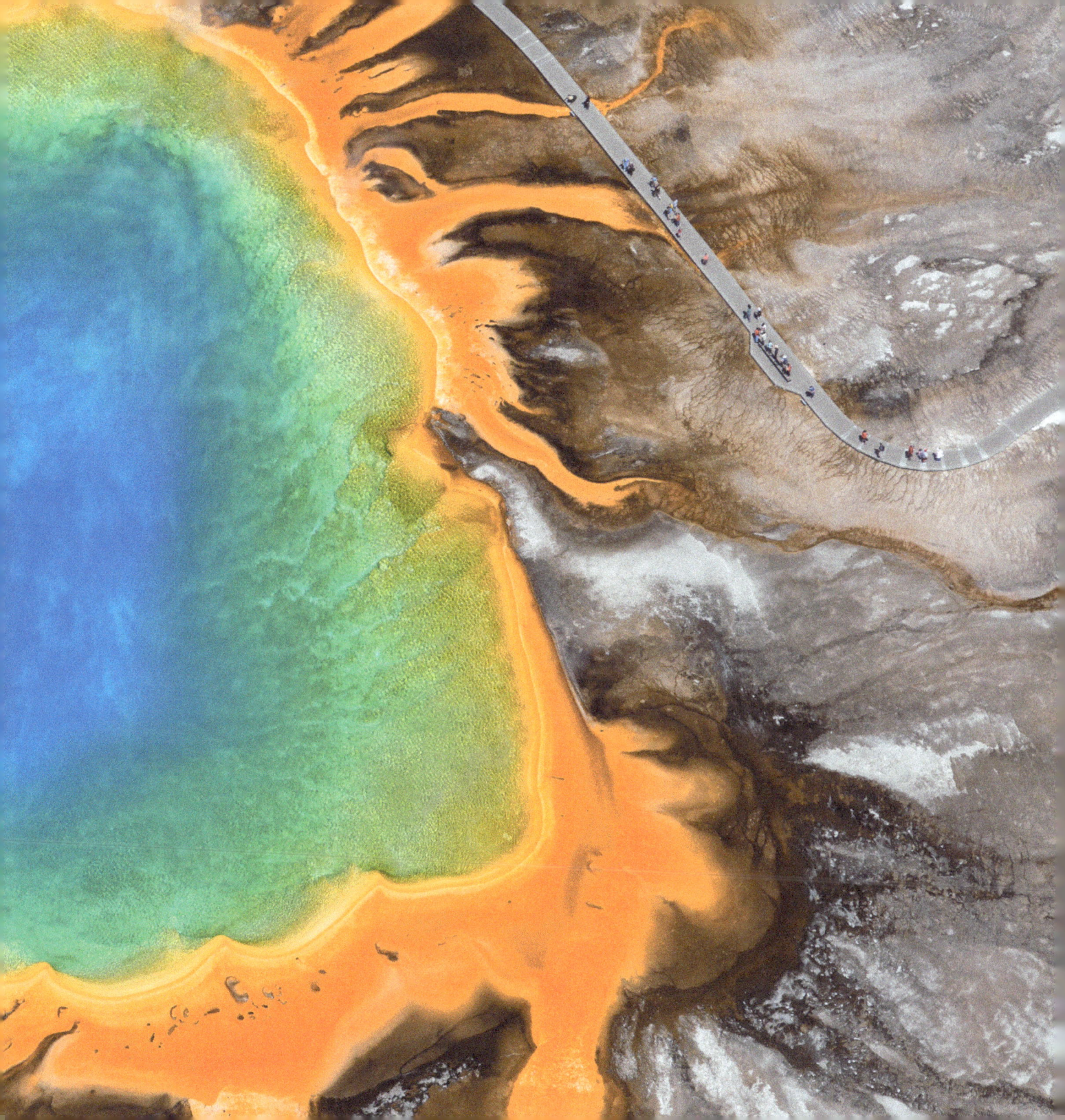

The state of Wyoming has a rich history. While it is not the most populous state in the country, it is rich in history. Here are some facts about Wyoming for kids that will help them learn more about the state.

In addition to the natural resources and the early progressivism, Wyoming is also home to colorful characters. In short, these facts will make learning about this state more fun! You can use these facts to teach children about this fascinating state.

Milton Keynes UK
Ingram Content Group UK Ltd.
UKHW050604240823
427303UK00009B/71